Shylock Reasons with Mr Chesterton by Humbert Wolfe

Humbert Wolfe CB CBE was born on 5th January 1885 in Milan, Italy from Jewish family roots.

Wolfe was brought up in Bradford, West Yorkshire and was a pupil at Bradford Grammar School before attending Wadham College at the University of Oxford.

Beginning at the Board of Trade and then the Ministry of Labour, Wolfe's career was in the Civil Service, where he achieved positions of high responsibility.

He was also one of the most popular and prolific authors of the 1920's and 30s across some 40 works, mainly poetry but including other genres. Indeed, Gustav Holst set a number of his verses to song in his 12 Humbert Wolfe Songs, Op. 48 (1929).

In 1931 he became a Fellow of Royal Society of Literature and was one of the favourites to become the next Poet Laureate where he was up against Rudyard Kipling, W.B.Yeats and the eventual occupant-to-be of the post Robert Bridges. Wolfe was also a noted translator including that of Heinrich Heine, Edmond Fleg and Eugene Heltai (Heltai Jenő).

In 1938 Wolfe was appointed Deputy Secretary to the Ministry of Labour and his main responsibility was to equip the country's labour force for the approaching Second World War. His duties then extended to drawing up a list of writers who could better serve as propagandists rather than soldiers in the British Army.

Although Wolfe was married, he engaged in a decade long affair with the novelist Pamela Frankau which ended only with his death.

Humbert Wolfe CB CBE died on 5th January 1940 at 75 Eccleston Square in London. It was his 55th birthday.

I0158437

Index of Contents

DEDICATION

Only this—that when I've done with wearing
Gold words upon my heart and reaching after
My immortality, I shall be hearing
Then, and long afterwards (be sure!) your laughter.

Only this—that when I come to sleeping
And later men appraise me in the quarrels
Of poets and the bays, tell them I'm keeping
No bays, but at my heart a lover's laurels.

SHYLOCK REASONS WITH MR. CHESTERTON

Jew-baiting still! Two thousand years are run
And still, it seems, good Master Chesterton,
Nothing's abated of the old offence.
Changing its shape, it never changes tense.
Other things were, this only was and is.
And whether Judas murder with a kiss,
Or Shylock catch a Christian with a gin,
All all's the same—the first enormous sin
Traps Judas in the moneylender's mesh
And cuts from Jesus' side the pound of flesh.
Nor is this all the punishment. For still
Through centuries to suffer were no ill
If we in human axes and the rod
Discerned the high pro-consulate of God
Chastening his people. But we are not chastened.
Age after age upon our hearts is fastened
The same cold malice, and for all they bleed
They burn for ever with unchanging greed.
Grosser with suffering we grow, and one
Calls to another "If in Babylon
Are gold and silver, be content with them,
Better found gold than lost Jerusalem."
They forget Zion; in the market place
Rebuild the Temple for the Jewish race,
And thus from age to age do Jews like me
Have their revenge on Christianity,
Since thus from age to age Christians like you
Unchristian grow in hounding down the Jew.
And thus from age to age His will is done,
And Shylock's sins produce a Chesterton.

But since we both must suffer and both are
Bound in the orb of one outrageous star,
Hater and hated, for a little while
Let us together watch how mile on mile
The heavenly moon, all milky white, regains
Her gentle empery, and smooths the stains
Of red our star left in her heaven, thus
Bringing a respite even unto us
Before the red star strikes again. The riot
Of the heart for a moment sinks, and in the quiet
Like a cool bandage on the forehead be
Content a second with tranquillity.
And from your lips the secular taunt of dog

Banish, to hear what in the synagogue
We heard once at Barmitzvah (as we call
The confirmation, when the praying shawl
Is for the first time worn, and the boy waits
For law and manhood at the altar gates).
Whether 'tis true or no, it shall be true
just long enough to build a bridge to you,
That hangs a shining second till your laughter
Reminds me of my ducats and my daughter.

It happened thus. When the last "adonoi"
Had faltered into silence of some boy
Whose voice was all a silver miracle
Of water, a voice echoed "Israel,"
A sweeter voice than even his, but broken
With a sorrowful thrill, as though the heart had spoken
Of countless generations doomed to pain
And none to ease them found. It cried again,
Or so we thought who listened, "Ye do well
To let the children come, O Israel,
But even these are lost and unforgiven,
Since not of these His kingdom and His heaven
Who at their fathers' fathers' hands was sold
In Calvary; and not their voice, though gold,
Nor innocent eyes, nor ways that children have
Of magic in their reaching hands, can save.
For, though ye offer these as sacrifice,
A nation's childhood is too small a price
To pay the interest upon the debt
That all your sorrows cannot liquidate.
O what a usury our God has made
On thirty pieces that the high priest paid!
Profit was none, but from the first the loss
That grew of the fourth ghost upon the Cross.
Two on the Cross were seen at Jesus' side,
The fourth, the fourth unseen and crucified
With piercéd hands and feet, and heart as well,
The ghost betrayed of traitor Israel.
Yourselves ye bought and sold, yourselves decreed
To the end of the world your doom. For who will heed
The prayer or utter mercy on a child,
However sweet he call? The heart is wild
Of your own ghost, and not the softest lamb
Of God escapes his sentence. For I am
The wraith of all your children from the first
Long ere their birth inexorably cursed."
None saw the ghost. Some said it was the boy
That spoke. Yet someone answered "adonoi,

Thy will be done" and it was finished. All
Closer about their foreheads drew the shawl
Fearing to see, and as the darkness grows
Deeper save where above the altar glows
One lamp, in hearts that Pharoah would unharden
For pity rises not a cry for pardon,
But to the Mills of God a bitter call
"Grind quickly, since ye grind exceeding small!"

That is the tale. But mark, the moon in heaven
Is hid with clouds. This little time was given
To peace and to remembering one another
Who might have been (God knows) brother with brother.
But since 'tis over and the peace is done
Shylock returns and with him Chesterton.

THE UNKNOWN GOD

"Whom you ignorantly worship, him I declare unto you."

I

PHEIDIAS

Pheidias, the sculptor, dying bade them set
His last-cut marble near lest he forget,
Travelling, where beauty ends, what beauty is
In the world and the light no longer his.
And while they brought it, women, as they use,
Sang in the house the litany of Zeus
That is the god of gods, yet could not save
His own beloved lady from the grave.
"The dearest head" they sung, "yea even her's,
Whose hair was like a harp, when the wind stirs
Upon the strings and wakes them, golden hair,
Must droop upon the ground and perish there—
Even her hair (the women sung), alas
For loveliness! wherein Olympus was
Lost for a god and found, when he, with mist
About him of its glory twist on twist,
Found on her mouth, more passionate for this,
Mortality, that trembled in the kiss
—Even that hair, for all a high god's art,
Long since is dust, and dust that was her heart."
This song of ending in the darkness came
To Pheidias in the courtyard, where the flame

Of torches threw a final light and shewed
Two pillars of the house, a turn of road
That led (he thought) beyond all sight, and he
Must walk it with a quiet company
—The cold imagined gods, no prayer might cozen
To help him on the way, immortal, frozen
Glimpses of deity his hand, creating
In marble out of his heart where they were waiting
For life, had carved, and given them instead
Of life the eternal gesture of the dead.
He with those gods must walk, since he had grown
Into their silence, and had made his own
Their longings thus imprisoned, and their heart
On one beat fixed for ever. He must start
To follow, but before his striving spirit
Steps out upon the road or falters near it,
One god, that guards the passage, waiting stands—
His latest marble, made like those, with hands,
Fashioned, like those, of a man's dreams, but overstepping
His maker's mind, and into a glory sweeping
No man might share. For the great forehead lifted
Out of the shade of life, and light had shifted
Her quality, whose radiant indecision
Found, though the eyes were closed, consummate vision.
This was the god that dying Pheidias
Had beaten out of marble. This he was,
And would not share with other gods their death
In beauty, but was living with the breath
Of his creator, who with death at strife
Laid down his own to give his creature life.
This god they brought to Pheidias, for whom
The whole great world had been a little room,
Which he had used, as others use, but he
Looked through the window on eternity.
And seeing his god, upon his mind the cloud
Faded an instant, and he cried aloud,
As though all Hellas heard him, "O be proud
Of beauty, Hellas, nor be curious
Of what the secret is that haunted us
Your poets, who had strained to it, and after
Lay down to sleep, sealing their lips with laughter.
For laughter is the judgment of the wise,
Who measure equally with level eyes
What the world is, what gods, and what are men,
And twixt too great a joy, too sharp a pain,
Strikes on a balance, so that tears are shot
With laughter, laughter with tears, and these are not
Themselves, but greater than themselves, and each

From other learns and doth to other teach.
We are content with beauty thus, who find
That when all's done—sculpture or song—behind
What we have carved or sung, a greater thing
Startles the heart with movement of a wing
We neither see nor dare see. For our thought
Is larger than we know, and what we sought
Passes and has forgotten; what we do,
The truth we did not guess at pierces through,
If what was done was well done. This last bust
Of mine not as I willed but as I must
I carved, and now, at the end of all, I can
See that the dream he does not dream is man.
The earlier gods I carved and knew, they wait
My coming as their master at the gate
Of death, for what I knew is mine to have,
Live with my life, and wither in my grave.
Thus beauty known is fading, known love fades,
And the truth we know a shadow in the shades,
And only that which lies beyond our hands,
Beauty, no earth-bound spirit understands,
But guesses at and faints for in desire;
And love, that does not burn, because the fire
Is lit beyond the world, and truth that dies
Beyond our thoughts in unimagined lies
That are the truth beyond truth, only these
Are lasting and outwit our memories.
But the familiar gods that I have made—
With those I will not walk. O be afraid
Of beauty attainable and love attained
And limited immortality. Unchained
The greatest soul must walk and walk alone
With what it has not seen and has not known!"
Thus Pheidias spoke and presently the flame
Of torches died, his god that had no name
—His latest statue—watched his spirit pass
And the dawn came that knew not Pheidias.

II

PAUL

Paul the apostle, on the sacred hill
Of Mars at Athens, felt a hidden will
Working against his gospel. That was old
(It seemed), yet had the thrust of boyhood cold,
Yet tempered in wild fires, and sensing this

He prayed in silence. The Acropolis,
Making a final bid for beauty, took
The dying sun to her heart with the wild look
As of a woman yielding to her lover;
And he in flame confederate leaning over
With armfuls of clouded roses, blossom on blossom,
Rifled the sweets of evening, and for her bosom
Dismantling heaven's high pavilion
With tumbled beauties wooed her thus and won.

This Paul from prayer rising saw, nor cared,
Watching a Cross in the East, if these had snared
The West with meshes trailing from the wrist
Of Venus, also an Evangelist.
"So little is the conquest of the flesh,
So like a spinner, weaving her small mesh
—And a boy tears it as he passes by—
Embroiders fruitlessly her tapestry
The Paphian woman, and the threads are thin
And ghostly as the new light enters in—
The tapestry that was the world and all
The curtain Jesus tears aside" says Paul:
"What is there worshipful here? These skies are fleeting,
This beauty made by hands of the sun is beating
Into the night that swallows her, and none
Is warm, when night has fallen, with the sun;
And the whole frame of the celestial
Firmament, though dusted with the stars, must fall
As being under death, and change in Hell,
When death is conquered, her corruptible
Beauty, and at the trumpet's sound put on,
As ye must also, incorruption."
And while he spoke the curtain of the sky
Night fretted with the cool embroidery
Of stars, and the moon upon her silent spindle
Did all the velvet warp to silver kindle.
But a young man of the philosophers,
Who stood about him, said "The moonlight stirs
With beauty in the heart, and in the mind
The things that seem do such a glory find
Lit with this wonder of the moon and star,
As almost to persuade us that they are,
But these we know are broken images
Of patterns laid-up in heaven. Socrates,
A citizen of Athens, was betrayed
To death for teaching this, and smiling laid
His cup of hemlock down, because his heart
Already of eternity was part,

And death for such is freedom. Yet for this
He did surrender the Acropolis,
That had all Hellas for a coronet
About her forehead radiantly set,
Island on island, and for this forsook
The friendship of his friends, his dreams, the look
Of hesitating spring that dare not stay
Yet will not leave the hills of Attica.
For this all gifts, all memories, he gave
Freely believing that the narrow grave
Was the end of all. Thus he passed out alone,
Content to face the gods no man had known
Because they beggar knowledge, and persuaded
It was enough, that, when for him had faded
The light, for us his death a light had lit
Would shew a path and we might walk by it.
'This is the spirit of man; in vain it reaches
Beyond the limits ordained and vainly stretches
To where truth, beauty, goodness, three in one,
Find each in all supreme communion.
For what is greater than we know,' he said
'It is well to die,' and smiling he was dead.
This he believed, all this he sacrificed.
Did he teach better, Jew, whom you call Christ?"

A cloud passed by the moon, and no one spoke,
Till suddenly her silver spear-head broke
The cloudy targe, and leaning from the place
She has in heaven struck with light the face
Of Pheidias' god. And Paul cried "Even thus
Ye have your answer, superstitious
Who set this idol up, and worshipped it
In darkness, and behold the face is lit
With fire from on high. A period
Is set to ignorance and to the god
Ye ignorantly worship, and the stone
Or marble of the god ye have not known,
Changes beneath my hand and in my speech
Unto the living god I know and preach.
Do you rejoice because that Socrates
Died facing death and dark? I tell you these
In Christ are conquered. Death has lost her sting,
The dark her victory, and angels sing
At the empty mouth of the grave, because my king
Has made the grave a refuge and protection
From the pain of living by His resurrection.
Socrates sleeps; the god he did not know
Sleeps with him, and long since the grasses grow

Above their resting place, but flowers reach
In vain their roots to find Him whom I preach.
He is not there, but though we darkly see,
As in a glass, his immortality
Waits for us all, and beckons in the place
Where we who find Him see Him face to face.
Socrates, to death a prisoner, did well,
But death was all; Christ by the miracle
Of the open grave, his deity forsaken,
For all the world has death a prisoner taken.
Nor Socrates in vain all sacrificed
If here his fruitless death has pled for Christ."
Dionysius the Areopagite
Cried loudly unto Paul "Were it not right
To shatter on his marble pedestal
This idol that has stood for death?" and Paul
Answered "What say ye brethren, for His sake
Who vanquished death shall we the idol break?"
But even as Paul raised his hand the light
Faded upon the sculptured face. The night
Cloaked it, and, though Paul pressed, the threatened blow
Hung in the air and fell not. For a low
Strange glory changed upon the face, and seemed
A face that Paul had seen before or dreamed
To see when near Damascus, and instead
Of Pheidias' god unknown another Head
Sorrowful-sweet on Paul astonished shone
And, ere his threatening hand could fall, was gone.
But a voice whispered "Art thou after all
Thine unknown God still persecuting, Saul?"

CASSIO HEARS OTHELLO

Thus for the last last time with the first kiss!
O my white bird, here is the precipice!
I throw you like a homing carrier
Into the footless spaces of the air!
And your spread wings, set free, beat up and out
In mounting circles, storming death's redoubt
And the cloudy fortress of Avilion.
Gone, my white bird, beyond all dreaming, gone!
And my hands warm that held her. Cassio
It was well done! Always to let her go
In the grave they shall be open thus, and yet
Feeling the half-poised wings—poor hands! Forget
My madness, Cassio, and think of me

As of a man who set his sea-bird free
From the prison of his heart to see her win
The deep blue floors of heaven and enter in.
O I am glad, I am glad, I dared this thing.
Even now my bird is home, awakening
Among her shining sisters, far—so far,
Not even the thoughts I have can trouble her.
So carve upon the stone that marks my grave:
"All that he had to death Othello gave,
And has kept nothing back but the sweet wound
Of life, that grew so dear, because he found
The mortal knife, that stabbed him, slit the strings
That gave his bird the guerdon of her wings."

THE FIRST AIRMAN

Give me the wings, magician. I will know
What blooms on airy precipices grow
That no hand plucks, large unexpected blossoms,
Scentless, with cry of curlews in their bosoms,
And the great winds like grasses where their stems
Spangle the universe with diadems.
I will pluck those flowers and those grasses, I,
Icarus, drowning upwards through the sky
With air that closes underneath my feet
As water above the diver. I will meet
Life with the dawn in heaven, and my fingers
Dipped in the golden floss of hair that lingers
Across the unveiled spaces and makes them colder,
As a woman's hair across her naked shoulder.
Death with the powdered stars will walk and pass
Like a man's breath upon a looking-glass,
For a suspended heart-beat making dim
Heaven brighter afterwards because of him.

Give me the wings, magician. So their tune
Mix with the silver trumpets of the moon
And, beyond music mounting, clean outrun
The golden diapason of the sun.
There is a secret that the birds are learning
Where the long lanes in heaven have a turning
And no man yet has followed; therefore these
Laugh hauntingly across our usual seas.
I'll not be mocked by curlews in the sky;
Give me the wings magician, or I die.

His call for wings or death was heard and thus
Came both to the first airman, Icarus.

MARY

(Sister of Martha)

There was no star in the East the night I came
With spikenard in hushed Jerusalem—
But a light in an upper chamber dimly lit
Was star enough—I would have followed it
Through lonelier streets unto the smaller room
Where afterwards it blossomed in the tomb.
Light of the world, but how much more to me
The light that other women also see!
No choiring angels in gold groups adored
Their king that night, but searching for my Lord
Unchoired, uncrowned, whose Kingdom had not come,
I heard none call, but dumb, as death is dumb,
The night misled his angels, or may be
Night and the angels made a way for me.
My footfalls in the street rang very clear
As I drew on. It seemed that all must hear
My coming, eyes that peered behind the grating,
Cloaked hands to hold me at each corner waiting.
But nothing stirred till suddenly there ran
The flame of the moon in heaven for a span
Less than a heart-beat, and I saw a man
Steal out of Simon's house, and pass me by
With such a horror on his lips that I,
Also a traitor, shrunk and knew him not—
Him that was Judas called Iscariot.
Also a traitor I, because I came
Not worshipping the Master in that Name
That his disciples called him, not the Christ
Of God for me that night. I sought a tryst
With a man of men, and if my heart had won
The Son of God had died in Mary's son,
And he, who, knowing the appointed evil,
Sent forth Iscariot to his task, a devil,
Also accepted, though this was more hard,
The sweet betrayal of the spikenard.
He knew me what I meant and in his eyes,
That for a moment smiled, was Paradise
Lost unto love, that for the greater sin
Than even Judas' might not enter in.

And when the disciples would have stayed my hands,
"She does but good" He said "she understands."
And I who poured the unguent understood,
But good it was not, as a man means good.
For I forget the Master, I but see
(A woman taken in adultery
With a dream and a dream) his human face
I would have saved from God, and in the place
Of Gospel and of resurrection I
Hear him say "Mary" and behold him die.
Judas, to death who sold him for a kiss,
Sinned less than I, who'd buy him back for this.
And Christ forgave me—How shall I forgive
Jesus, my love, the man who would not live?

THE SICILIAN EXPEDITION

To-day the Triremes sailed for Sicily
With no wind stirring on a soundless sea;
But a great crying of birds beat up and filled
The empty caverns of the air and stilled
The thrashing of the oars. The level sun
Unto himself, it seemed, drew one by one
With strings of gold the ships that no one heard
Move on the waters, till at last one bird
(Of all the wings past knowledge and past counting)
Wheeled upwards on the air and mounting, mounting,
Rose out of human sight, but all the rest
Passed with the passing fleet into the West.

To-day the Triremes sailed—and will their sailing
Prosper or fail because a gull was wailing
For crumbs about the prows? Who but a fool
Would find a message in a screaming gull?
For if gods use such messengers as these
The less gods they (or so says Socrates).
They are not gods (he says) of fear and hate,
A swollen type of man degenerate,
Catching at flattery, at sorrow fleering
And every spiteful whisper overhearing;
But largely on their mountain they attend
Unflinchingly the one appointed end,
When what was nobly done and finely striven
Will find the archetype laid up in heaven.
Not these by gulls pronounce or suffer doom,
Nor cries among the ships (and yet the gloom

Settles about Athene's temple. If
An injured god used his prerogative
Of anger, might not Hermes?)—that's the gull
Stirring the superstition of a fool!
What if a week ago we, waking, found
The Hermae spoiled or fallen to the ground?
Shall Fate be altered or a doom be spoken
Because an image was in malice broken?
Or Athens, that remembers Marathon,
Rock in her empire for a splintered stone?
How dear she is—was never city else
So loved, or lovely in her strength; like bells
Pealed in the brain her beauty. This is she,
Athens, whose sweeter name is liberty.

To-day the Triremes sailed—as Zeus decrees
All shall be done; but hardly Socrates,
As Westward in the dark our captains wear,
Would frown if an Athenian spoke a prayer
Even to Hermes, (even though it seem
We fear the flight of birds and cries in him),
Thus saying simply for the love of her—
Athens—"O Hermes, called the Messenger,
God of the wings, since now the sails are set,
If aught was evil, evil now forget!
If aught was left undone, think not of this
But her remember, Hermes, what she is,
A city leaning to the sea, and shod
With freedom on her feet, as thou a god
With wings art poised for flight—O, if the gull
Were bird of thine, Hermes, be merciful."

CAESAR AND ANTHONY

Augustus Caesar, aging by the sea,
Remembered, musingly, dead Anthony,
And wondered as he thought upon his days
Which had been better, laurel leaves or bays.
"Bays for the victor, when his fight is over,
But laurels" thought Augustus "for the lover.
That brown Egyptian woman, the fierce queen
Who with a serpent died—she came between
Him and the world's dominion, whispering
'Does empire burn so, has thy crown the sting
These lips have when they touch thee—thus and thus?
Choose then!' 'I choose!' replied Antonius."

"I wonder" thought Augustus as he lay
Watching the menial clouds of conquered day
Applaud with vehement reflection
The cold triumphant ending of the sun.
"The sun's an emperor, and all the sky
Burns to a flame for his nativity,
And not less beautiful nor unattended
By conquered flocks of cloud he passes splendid,
Throwing his slaves this laminated gold.
Master in death, but in his death how cold!
But to have died astonished on a kiss
Had heat to the end and Anthony had this."

THE DANCERS

This was the way of it, or I forget
How visions end. The flaming sun was set
Or setting in a sky as green as grass,
Stained here and there like a window, where there was
A martyr-cloud with halo dipped in gold
Or red as the Sacred Heart is. From the old
Low house—a country house not built with hands
And of that country where the poplar stands
Whose leaves have shivered in our dreams—there came
With the rising moon the dancers to the same
Tune we have heard we scarce remember when,
Nor care so only that it sound again.
Each dancer wears a fancy for a dress,
This one with starlike tears is gemmed no less
Than that is crowned with roses as of lips
That kissed and do not kiss. There also trips
Pierrot, because we all have lost, and thin,
Cruelly swift, victorious Harlequin,
Because some find and keep, but both entwine,
Because she needs them both, with Columbine.
Then lanterns on the trees to radiant fruit
Burn till dawn plucks them, and the light pursuit
Of dancers on the lawn is done, and laughter
Of those who fled and those who followed after
Dies; to a little wind the darkened trees
Bend gravely and resume their silences.

I have always known just where the river ends
(Or seems to end) that I shall find my friends,
Who are my friends no longer, being dead,
And hear the ordinary things they said,
That now seem wonderful, some evening when
I take the Number Nineteen bus again
To Battersea. It will, I think, be clear
With stars behind the four great chimneys. Dear
In the moon, young and unchanging, they
Will cry me welcome in the boyish way
They had before they went to France, but I,
A boy no more, will greet them silently.

THE WOODCUTTERS OF HÜTTELDORF

"The plan by which individual Viennese are allowed to obtain their own wood supplies has already been described by more than one observer. It will, however, in time to come appear so incredible, and it so completely sums up the misery of the people and the breakdown of civilization and administration, that no excuse is needed for placing it once more formally and definitely on record.

In the immediate neighbourhood of Vienna lies a forest known as the Wienerwald, the nearest point being on hills to the north, two or three miles from the centre of the city.

The two chief centres of wood collection are the suburbs of Hütteldorf and Dorhbach.

The prevalence of women and children among the collectors is the most painful feature of the proceedings."

From "Peace in Austria," by Sir W. Beveridge.

Nous n'irons plus au bois: the woods are shut:
Les lauriers sont coupés: the laurels cut.
Thus love, when still his pitiful sweet cry
For youth and spring, his play-boys, sensibly
Touched at the heart. But now he does not care
What woods, what trees are standing anywhere.
For there's no wood in the world to be found
That does not stab his feet, and the trees wound
His eyes with thorns—the eyes which did not see
In joy, but find their sight in misery.

There is a wood they named the Wienerwald.
There when the spring was new the throstle called
Spring to her ball-room, and the Viennese
Heard her light foot provoking the grave trees,
Half willingly at first, young leaves to stir,

That later passionately danced with her.
And here the cannon-fodder used to feed
The altar-fire of the older need,
And sweeter than the need of death. In spring
The Austrian boys saw love awakening
Here, and as English boys in English wood
Have given all to love, all that they could
These gave—their childhood, dawn's relentless star
That is put out with kisses. These they gave
And buried childhood lightly in her grave
So that a man might hear her calling yet,
"Primrose farewell, good-morrow violet!"—
Might yet have heard her, but the woods are shut
To those who would return: the laurels cut.

There are many go to-day to Wienerwald,
But love does not go with them. He has failed
In the Great War, who had so little skill
In the Will to Murder, love who was the Will
To live and make live, but the War has shewn
His Will is treachery, and love's alone
In a great wilderness. For if he cries
Aloud, they mock him in their Paradise—
The Angels of Armageddon. "This is he
Who ruled us, being blind, now let him see"
They say, "a prisoner, what we have done,
The priests of mankind's last religion.
Let him look deep and celebrate in Hell
How we reverse the Christian miracle,
Stealing their spirits from the sullen swine
And consecrating them as yours and mine,
So that we rush together suddenly
Down a steep place, where by an empty sea
Our worshippers pile on a flaming wharf
The trees that were the woods at Hütteldorf."

Ares, the god of battles, has prevailed.
At Hütteldorf, deep in the Wienerwald,
They go to the woods for fuel, and one sees
A child that beats upon the laurel trees
With starved small hands that hold an axe, and how
The spring returns to find a hooded crow
Waiting and waiting, as the thrush once waited
For childhood's end. But this, it seems, was fated
That all should change, save only that these seem
Still unsubstantial as the lover's dream,
As unsubstantial, but with blossoms set
That have no traffic with the violet

And primrose. Here the purple flowers of Dis
Burn their young foreheads and they fade with this,
Who find a different end and different haven,
Where the hooded crow is waiting with the raven.

In Wienerwald the starving Viennese
Have spoiled the woods and cut the laurel trees,
Nous n'irons plus au bois: oh love, oh love!
Will you not go the more because they prove
So shattered, the poor woods? and will you shut
Your heart, O love, because the trees are cut?
Les lauriers sont coupés, but you can heal
Even the broken laurel, and reveal
Where in the valley of death the children falter
That, though all else doth change, love does not alter,
And, though the woods were dead, there is a tree
You know of, love, planted in Calvary.

Go back to the woods; replant the laurel trees.
Still love than war hath greater victories,
And while the devils beat the warlike drum
Into their kingdom of peace the children come.

HEINE'S LAST SONG

Life's a blonde of whom I'm tired
(Being fair is just a knack
Women learn to be desired
By a Jew—who answers back).

Blonde, oh blonde, ye lost princesses
With the shadow in your eyes
As of bodiless caresses
Known ere birth in Paradise.

Little ears of alabaster,
Where like ocean in a shell
Gentle murmurs drown the vaster
Voice of rapture or of Hell.

Tender bodies—ah too tender
To be given or be lent
Unto love the money-lender
Who demands his cent per cent.

Thus you took a man and tricked him,

Life and ladies, to a will
In your favour, but the victim
Cheats you with a codicil.

All I had, you thought, was given—
Life and ladies, you were wrong:
In a poet's secret heaven
There is always one last song.

Even he is half afraid of,
Even he but hears in part,
For the stuff that it is made of,
Ladies, is the poet's heart.

Not for you, oh blonde princesses
Is that final tune, but I
Sing it drowning in the tresses
Of a darker Lorelei.

For her hair than yours is stranger;
Wilder lights are lost in hers
Where the heart's immortal danger,
That you cannot know of, stirs.

Life and ladies, it is over:
Blonde asks all, gives nothing back;
You must find another lover,
For the poet chooses black.

Where death's raven marriage blossom
Falls in clouds about her breast,
On his dark beloved's bosom
Heinrick Heine is at rest.

IMPERSONALITIES

THE SATYR

"Hollow" he cries and "hollow, hollow."
Mark how the creeping moon is yellow
On the cold stones, enmeshing feet
That are not soft, with blood not sweet.

Though in the night one cry his Name
The shuddering air shrinks from the aim;
And failing eddies will not stir

To let him through to Lucifer.

What answers where no echoes fly?
None where the moon looks balefully.
Unheard, far-off "O hollow, hollow"
The satyr crieth to his fellow.

BALDER'S SONG

It may be raining now, that first warm rain
That melts the heart of earth beneath the snows,
Our Northland snows (she feels the swimmer's pain
Who catches breath, half-drowned, when the blood flows
Shuddering back into the frozen vein).
And did ye think I should not come again
At the long last in spring-time with the rain?

Or may be there is singing in the air
At building-time where the tall windy trees,
By sap and young leaves hurt, can hardly bear
The spring's reiterated urgencies
That at the woods with actual fingers tear.
And did ye, when these songs are everywhere,
Of Balder, who first taught them song, despair?

Or it may be where once my altar stood
And where my worshipped name in prayer ascended,
Blue, like a trumpet, in the solitude
Harebells, that ring before the winter's ended,
Have with the wind my litanies renewed.
Did ye forget (alas! that any could)
That I, the god of flowers, found these good?

And may be where the dog-rose remedies
With her wild flush the hedge, and spring begins,
Born of all these there trembles the first kiss
That from Valhalla brings the Paladins
And ladies, who for all the immortal bliss
Of heaven, have no joy as sharp as this.
Did ye not know in your own memories
That where are love and spring there Balder is?

It may be raining now, that first warm rain
That melts the heart of earth beneath the snows,
Our Northland snows (she feels the swimmer's pain
Who catches breath, half-drowned, when the blood flows

Shuddering back into the frozen vein).
And did ye think I should not come again
At the long last in spring-time with the rain?

MARY THE MOTHER

(Cradle Song)

So great a lady, so dear is she,
Princess in heaven, but mother to me!
When little Jesus lay in her arm
It was enough for him that he was warm.

When the small head at her bosom did nod
Did she remember that He was the God?
Or when she sang to Him low in His ear,
Did she say "Master" or did she sob "Dear"?

Was it the star on the manger that shone
Crowned her an empress, or was it her Son?
So great a lady to lie in a stall—
But only a mother (she thought) after all.

So great a lady, so dear is she,
Princess in heaven! but who does not see
How against Godhead, in spite of the Cross,
She holds to her bosom her Jesus that was?

APPLES

When there is no more sea and no more sailing
Will God go vintaging the wine-dark seas,
Reaping gold apples of the storm and trailing
To harvest home the lost Hesperides?

Will God, the gates that guard the river breaking,
Annul the blinding gesture of the sword,
And find the Tree, all other dreams forsaking,
Whose apples are the knowledge of the Lord?

Forsaking dreams—forgiveness and salvation,
Sins that were needless needlessly forgiven,
Hell where he knew vicarious damnation
And ghosts of rapture in a ghost of heaven?

No longer from self-knowledge then exempted
Shall God the apple tasting Eve repeat
Thus altered, saying, "By the devil tempted
Through all these years I could and did not eat."

Thus at the last shall Man and Maker pardon
Eve's ancient wrong, seeing that, though He cursed,
Knowledge, alone of those who used the Garden
God was afraid of apples from the first.

Thereafter as it was in the beginning,
Before the spirit moved upon the deep,
There shall be no more sea and no more sinning
And God will share with his beloved sleep.

THE SKIES

Though the world tumble tier by tier,
Down, down the broken galleries,
By day the sun would shine as clear
By night the moon would ride her seas.

Though man and all was meant by men
Upon the empty air were spent,
Irrevocably Charles's Wain
Would swing across the firmament.

So large they are and cool the skies;
God's frozen breath in dreams, or worse:
Beautiful unsupported lies
That simulate a universe.

THREE EPITAPHS

I

FLECKER

You have made the golden journey. Samarkand
Is all about you, Flecker, and where you lie
How youth and her beauty perish in the sand
They are singing in the caravanserai.

II.

EDITH CAVELL

Who died for love, we use to nourish hate:
Who was all tenderness, our hearts to harden;
And who of mercy had the high estate
By us escheated of her right of pardon.

III

THE LITTLE SLEEPER

This little sleeper, who was overtaken
By death, as one child overtakes another,
Dreams by his side all night and will not waken
Till the dawn comes in heaven with his mother.

TO HIM WHOM THE CAP FITS

*"What sword is left?" sighs England. Answer her
(For you must answer) "This—Excalibur."*

I

That is the sword of England. Arthur drew
The blade at that last battle when he failed,
(Shadow among the shadows, who prevailed
Victorious in disaster). Harold knew
Its point in his heart at Hastings, and it flew
Out of the scabbard when King Richard sailed
And did not reach Jerusalem. It wailed
In the false hand that on the scaffold slew
Charles, and proud Balliol saw the light on it
Shining for Ridley through the flame; was seen
When Mary, Queen of Scotland, was a queen
On earth no longer, and when William Pitt
"England! O how I leave thee," failing cried,
The sword, the sword, was with him when he died.

II

The line at Mons were privy to the blade,
When God and England seemed together lost,
And riding by the far Pacific coast

Admiral Cradock took its accolade.
These are its victories—to be afraid,
To hear thin bugles sounding "The Last Post,"
Until the blood creeps noiseless as a ghost
And cold, and all we cherished is betrayed.
That is the sword's way. Those who lose shall have;
And only those who in defeat have known
The bitterness of death, and stood alone
In darkness, shall have worship in the grave.
Swordsman, go into battle, and record
How one more English knight has found his sword!

FRANCE

To-day you'll find by field and ditch
The small invasion of the vetch:
And where they sleep rest-harrow will
Follow upon the daffodil.

These in their soft disordered ranks
Withstand and overcome the Tanks;
And the small unconsidered grass
Cries to the gunner "On ne passe."

The corn outlasts the bayonet,
Whose blades no blood nor rust can fret,
Or only the immortal rust
Of poppies failing in their thrust.

The line these hold no force can break,
Nor their platoons advancing shake,
Whose wide offensive wave on wave
Doth make a garden of a grave.

These with the singing lark conspire
To veil with loveliness the wire,
While he ascending cleans the stain
In heaven of the aeroplane.

These in the fields and open sky
Reverse the errors of Versailles,
Who with a natural increase
From year to year establish peace.

For all the living these will cloak
The things they spoiled, the hearts they broke;

And where these heal the earth will be
For all the dead indemnity.

ALCHEMY

When Kew found spring, and we found Kew,
Gold was the London that we knew—
The gold of gold whose metal is
As yellow as the primroses.

London's Lord Mayor, Dick Whittington,
In heaven heard the carillon
"Turn again;" London after all
Is paved with gold by Chiswick Mall.

But afterwards the town was sold
To a mad alchemist for gold,
Who used his art to change, instead
Of lead to gold, the gold to lead.

If where the streets to Hampstead twist
You meet a doting alchemist
Seeking lost gold, refuse him pity;
He changed us when he changed the city!

ORPHEUS

What Orpheus whistled for Eurydice
(While all the shades were silent, achingly
Holding out hands, and hands stretched evermore
In a vain longing for the further shore).

The blue smoke floats
Lazily in the dawn above the white
Flat roof you knew, and somewhere out of sight
A child is singing the old Linus song,
Sweeter because the baby voice goes wrong
—The little goatherd calling to her goats.

There's a small hill
On which the olive trees you used to call
Athene's little sisters, now grown tall,
Watch all day long the coming of the child,
And you'll remember how the brook, else wild,

About these pastures suddenly grows still.

There's such a peace,
Save where a wandering beast shakes on its bell,
You'd almost think the trees had learned a spell
From their wise sister (or from you) to bless
A baby frightened of the loneliness,
Tending her herd and waiting by the trees.

Ah! certainly
There are two things are stronger than the fates—
A lover's song in Hell, a child that waits.
The shadows lengthen. Ere the night descend
On earth, O sweetheart, Mother, friend
Win out of Hell! Return Eurydice!

THE WIND

What is there left? The wind makes answer
"I saw the green leaves grow brown and fall;
I danced with the shadows, I the dancer
Among bare branches. For I," he saith,
"Hear the thin music whistle and call,
Music, horn-music, the music of death."

"There stands at the edge of the wood the player
Dark in the darkness, but I have seen,
Ere my feet were lifted, the branches stir.
Darker than dark, than light more fair,
Before I have come he slips between;
But I, the dancer," wind saith, "do not care."

"The leaves have fallen and who shall discover
What there is left in the blackened tree?
And who will know when the years are over,
Among bare branches if I," wind saith,
"Dance where the shadows and music be,
Music, horn-music, the music of death?"

GABRIEL

Suppose I gave you what my heart has given—
A door to dreams, a little road to heaven.
Would you pass through the door, my dreams forgetting,

And turn the corner when my sun is setting?

So I should only have (as I have only)
Your hair remembered, eyes that left me lonely,
A mouth as cold as roses, and the kiss
Of Gabriel, sealing love's defeat with this!

OPALS AND AMBER

Call it an age, call it a day,
What's in the world with love away?
The sun a round and golden ghost,
The moon the shadow he has lost;
And spring herself for all her green
The bare and brown a pause between.
Call it an age, call it a day,
When love is gone, what's there to say?

Opal or gold, amber or gray,
What's in the world with love away?
Opal a pool of changeling fires,
Where the gold angel stirs desires
That do not heal Bethesda way
But only turn the amber gray.
Call it an age, call it a day,
When love is gone, what's there to say?

Call it a dream, call it a play,
What's in the world with love away?
With love away can a man clamber
To heaven by a rope of amber?
Or can an opal stretch a wire
To lead a girl to her desire?

Amber and opal—but I remember
Love that was better than opal or amber.
Call it an age, call it a day,
What's in the world with love away?

AFTER BATTLE

After the fighting
Comes not sudden peace, but weariness;
A gloom no lighting

Of little lamps of jest or speech unravels,
But for the brain and body endless travels,
Twisting and turning like the lovers hurled
For punishment athwart the underworld,
Twisting and turning and no respite sighting.

After the living
Comes not relief, but a grey level gloom,
When the heart beats as in a padded room
With wild shapes moving—
Silence imploring and from silence flying,
Praying to life and all athirst for dying.
Tearing lost dreams and for the torn dreams weeping,
Fearing to wake, tumultuously sleeping.

Death's a poor leech with worn-out simples striving
To heal in vain the malady of living.

MADEMOISELLE DE MAUPIN

When the stir and the movement are over,
When you that had the lightness of a wind
Or the poise of some swift bird
Burn no longer in any man's mind,
And your voice in no man's heart is heard,
Who in the world will dare to be a lover?

Would any being hurt in the night be crying
"O God! her little mouth that with a kiss
Drank all a man; and—God! her weaving fingers!"
Would any of another dare say this?
Will there be other women, other singers?
I wish with you and me love might be dying.

DU BIST WIE EINE BLUME

(Version)

You have the way of a blossom,
Cold petal with April green,
And you melt the heart in the bosom
As your beauty enters in.

I will fold my hands together,

Asking of God for you
Always in April weather
Cold petal and colder dew.

CAMBRIDGE

All that I know of Cambridge—
The colleges and that indulgent air
Of a great gentleman who is content
That lesser men should make experiment
With life, for which he does not vastly care—
Is that you tell me you were happy there.

All that I'll say of Cambridge—
Though in her courts Apollo lose the art
Of immortality to find it where
Rupert was used to walk at Grantchester—
Is that for me Cambridge is but a part
Of greater beauties than inform your heart.

A ROOM IN BOHEMIA

The sun is shining in the August weather
In the little room and, I suppose,
Gilding the painted parrot on the wall,
The truckle-bed, the table and the rose
Of the poor carpet that we bought together.
And from the street the muted voices call
As though we saw, as though we heard it all.

VICTORY

Let it be written down, while still the wound
Festers and there is horror in the world
At what was done and suffered, while unfurled
The wings of death are dark upon the ground.
Let it be written "Death we have not found
The worst, though death is evil, nor the curled
Fangs of disease, nor yet to ruin hurled
The tracery of old cities, when no sound

Is in their broken streets. But there's an ape

Out of the slime into the spirit creeping,
That twists mankind back, back into the shape
That mumbles carrion. Here's the cause for weeping.
Prognathous chin, slant forehead, eyes that rust
As their flame dies and smoulders into lust."

CLEOPATRA

Why should I care for love? The urgent rose—
What does she promise the heart and what fulfill?
"Delight, delight" she whispers, and she goes ...
But love the rose outbidding is falser still.

Why should I care for love? But hush, oh hush!
What bird is singing in the dawn "Forget
The spring," and, you,—have you forgotten, thrush?...
But love the thrush outsinging is falser yet.

Why should I care for love? Love does not care
Whether you care or do not care, says she!
But ask your lips how the rose smells in my hair,
If the thrush beats at my heart—here—Anthony!

MEDUSA

In your black hair are there not nightingales
Singing in the dark, and when you let it down
Is there no stir in the air of tiniest sails
That ever on lost seas of song were blown?

In your black hair the heart of Hyacinth
Laments the daylight he shall see no more,
And flowers are red as in the labyrinth
The red eyes of the crazy Minotaur.

In your black hair, Medusa, there are snakes
That twine themselves about Laocoon,
How soft, how warm! and how the poor heart breaks
Before they strike and turn it into stone.

THE JUNGLE

Truth is the fourth dimension. By her grace
Motion, the idiot of time and space,
Grows reasonable, so that the spirit sees
Behind the aimless drag of categories
The moving centuries, whose gestures mirror
And dissipate the cloudy shapes of error.
O there's the long way back, the dawns that scatter
Like startled birds about the spirit, and chatter
Of animal voices seeking lucid speech
In colonies of darkness. Truth can stretch,
Though motionless, and set a hatchet blazing
A path through the jungle where an ape is gazing
At the edge of a little light, with dripping muzzle,
Black writhing palms, and eyes a drowsy puzzle
Of fears and beastlike hopes. Then the light reaches
His pelt and holds him fast. In vain he snatches
At the sheltering trees, in vain the leafy dance
Down the long avenues of ignorance.
Knowledge and the pain of knowledge fly beside him,
And, where the leaves are darkest, clutch and ride him
Until he sloughs the shape of beast and can
Stand in the dawn upon his feet a man.

But the jungle is not cleared, and still the shapes
Of time and space and error move like apes.

THE PENCIL

With this golden pencil—write
"Written words must serve for sight.
For the broken lights that stirred
Wedded eyes the complete word.

Written words the trembling nerve
Of the lover's ear must serve.
Laughter's done and tears are over—
Written words, instead, my lover.

Words that have no scent must tell
How the secret jonquils smell
In your hair, and words protest
There are jonquils at your breast.

Written words the gift must waste,
When the very air hath taste
Of your lip, the sweets that part

Love's soft mouth and reach the heart.

Separable these await
For the fifth to consummate,
That are nothing, each alone,
But all heaven joined in one.

This, being lost, had hurt too much,
Here are words instead of touch."

Therefore write and break the lead
"Love that was alive is dead."

COLUMBINE

If any ask, O tell them that the moon
Was lit in heaven when Queen Ashtaroth
Beat at her lamp and fell upon the swoon
Of love that soars in fire to fall a moth.

If any ask, O tell them that for this
Priam's great city of Troy was sacrificed,
For love that is as bitter as the kiss
Of Judas the Iscariot, slaying Christ.

If any ask, O tell them it is well,
Though love comes like the swallow and flies as soon:
Who has not found his heaven in the Hell
Of love unsatisfied beneath the moon?

THE CROWDER'S TUNE

The crowder's tune
Down a street in Babylon—
His fiddle to the moon
With notes like stars that one by one
Glittered upon the empty street,
Glittered and laughed and went
(But there was a lisp of ghostly feet)
To build a firmament.

"Who walks by night in Babylon?
'I,' said a lady, 'because
Of the wonderful thing I was,

And the beautiful things all done,
I walk in Babylon.'

Who seeks for a lady by night?
'I,' said a king, 'My throne
Is empty in Babylon.
She fled from the light to the light,
I seek for a lady by night.'

Who calls by night in Babylon?
'They,' answered love, 'Yes over and over
She calls to her God, but he to his lover,
And each of them walks by night alone,
And they will not meet in Babylon.'"

The crowder played
His little tune, almost
As though he were afraid
Of some forgotten ghost
Awakening,
And crying on the string
Of what was lost
And would not come
Again.
He feared in vain.
For the ghost, the ghost is dumb
Of love that is past over,
And the merciless laughter of the moon
Pursues the ghostly lover,
Till in the empty street
There's an end of the lisp of feet,
And the crowder breaks his fiddle and the tune,
And all the stars are gone
In Babylon.

ENVOI

Past Buckhurst Hill the motor-bus
Takes and shakes the three of us.
When first we went, there were but two
In Epping Forest, I and you.

That summer as I understand
A forester from fairyland
Set a notice up, "No road,"
By the ways our feet had trod.

No one came and no one knew,
When the spring returned and blue
Flowers burned, how deep behind
Burned the blossoms of the mind.

No one guessed and no one heard
How beyond the singing bird,
Some one sang in solitude
In the wood within the wood.

No one watched the years go by
(Not even you, not even I),
In the wood alone apart
Green and waiting in the heart.

Till last week the forester
Heard a little footstep stir,
Took his notice down and smiled
At the coming of a child.

Conquering the solitude
A child is laughing in the wood.
Past Buckhurst Hill the motor-bus
Takes us back the three of us.

Humbert Wolfe – A Concise Bibliography

London Sonnets (1920)
Shylock Reasons with Mr. Chesterton and other poems (1920)
"Labour Ministry and Department of Labour (United Kingdom)" and "Labour Supply and Regulation (United Kingdom)" Encyclopedia Britannica, Vol. XXXI (1922)
Circular Saws (1923)
Labour Supply and Regulation (1923)
The Lilac (1924)
Lampoons (1925)
The Unknown Goddess (1925) Poems
Humoresque (1926)
News of the Devil (1926) Poems
Requiem (1927) Poems
Cursory Rhymes (1927) Poems
Others Abide (1927)
Kensington Gardens (1924)
Dialogues and Monologues (1928) Criticism
This Blind Rose (1928) Poems
Troy (1928) Ariel poems

The Moon and Mrs. Misses Smith (1928)
The Craft of Verse (1928) Essay
The Silver Cat and other poems (1928)
Notes on English Verse Satire (1929)
A Winter Miscellany (1930) Editor
Homage to Meleager (1930)
Tennyson (1930)
The Uncelestial City (1930)
Early Poems (1930)
George Moore (1931)
Snow (1931) Poems
Signpost to Poetry (1931)
Reverie of Policeman: A ballet in three acts (1933)
Now a Stranger (1933) Autobiography
Romantic and Unromantic Poetry (1933)
Truffle Eater. Pretty Stories and funny pictures (under the alias 'Oistros' with pictures by Archibald Louis Charles Savory (1933)
Portraits by Inference (1934)
Sonnets pour Helene (by Ronsard) (1934) Translator
X at Oberammergau: A poem (1935) Drama
The Fourth of August (1935) Poems
Selected Lyrics of Heinrich Heine (1935) Translator
P. L. M.: Peoples Landfalls Mountains (1936)
The Pilgrim's Way (1936)
The Silent Knight: A Romantic Comedy in Three Acts (by Eugene Heltai) (1937) Translator
Others Abide: Translated Greek Epigrams (1937)
The Upward Anguish (1938) Autobiography
Out of Great Tribulation (1939) Poems
Kensington Gardens in War-Time (1940) Poems